Macbook 1 for Seniors

A Clear, Practical Guide for Easy Learning

From Turning It On to Advanced Features – Learn How to Use Your Mac with Confidence

Kylan P.crook

Copyright © 2024 by Kylan P.crook

All rights reserved. This book is an original work and copyrighted publication, protected under the laws of the United kingdom. No part of this book, including its content or any other material, may be reproduced or transmitted in any form or by any means, including photocopying, recording, or other electronic or mechanical methods without the prior written permission of the copyright owner. The information provided in this book is intended for personal use and educational purposes only.

TABLE OF CONTENT

Introduction...... 4
Chapter 1: Getting Started with Your MacBook... 10
    1.1 Unboxing and Initial Setup...... 10
    1.2 Navigating the Setup Assistant...... 12
    1.3 Exploring the Desktop and Basic Features... 16
Chapter 2: Connecting to the Internet and Setting Up Accounts......20
    2.1 Connecting to Wi-Fi......21
    2.2 Setting Up Email Accounts......23
    2.3 Setting Up Apple ID and iCloud...... 25
Chapter 3: Navigating and Personalizing Your MacBook...... 30
    3.1 Understanding Finder and File Management 31
    3.2 Customizing the Desktop and System Preferences......33
    3.3 Installing and Managing Applications......36
Chapter 4: Communication and Staying Connected...... 41
    4.1 FaceTime and Video Calls...... 42
    4.2 Messages and Communication Apps....... 44
    4.3 Setting Up and Using Social Media......... 47
Chapter 5: Productivity and Everyday Apps.... 51
    5.1 Using Safari for Browsing the Web........... 52

5.2 Staying Organized with Calendar and Reminders...55
5.3 Taking Notes and Staying Organized........57
Chapter 6: Advanced MacBook Features......... 61
6.1 Introduction to Siri..................................... 62
6.2 iCloud and File Sharing.............................64
6.3 Security and Privacy Features.................. 67
Chapter 7: Troubleshooting and Maintenance. 71
7.1 Common Issues and Solutions................. 72
7.2 Regular Maintenance Tips........................ 74
7.3 Finding Additional Support........................77
Chapter 8: Tips and Tricks for Daily Use.......... 80
8.1 Time-Saving Tips...................................... 81
8.2 Accessibility Features............................... 84
8.3 Customizing Notifications and Alerts.........87
Appendix..90
Conclusion... 99

Introduction

Starting with a new device like a MacBook can feel overwhelming, and that's completely normal. In a world where technology changes so quickly, it's easy to feel lost, especially if you're unfamiliar with the latest gadgets. This guide is here to help you navigate your MacBook with ease, providing you with step-by-step guidance that feels as supportive as having a friend by your side. Think of this book as your personal tour guide, someone who understands that learning something new takes time and patience, especially when it comes to technology.

Whether you're a senior exploring the world of digital devices for the first time, a beginner transitioning from a different system, or simply someone who wants to get more out of their MacBook, you're in the right place.

This book was created with you in mind. Technology doesn't have to be intimidating, and it certainly doesn't require you to have any prior knowledge or special skills.

You might have just unboxed your MacBook, or maybe you've had it for a while but haven't felt comfortable diving into its features. Wherever you're starting from, this guide will meet you there. It's structured to be straightforward and welcoming, without the technical jargon that so often makes learning feel like a chore. This isn't about complex programming or advanced tech terminology; it's about making everyday tasks easier and helping you feel confident as you learn.

The book is organized in a way that lets you learn at your own pace. Each chapter focuses on a particular aspect of using your MacBook, moving from the basics to more advanced features as you become comfortable. The guide starts by helping you set up your device, so you'll be ready to go from the moment you turn it on. After that, you'll explore simple yet essential tasks, like connecting to Wi-Fi, sending emails, and customizing your desktop, which will help you start feeling at home on your Mac. As you continue, you'll learn about using the internet, organizing files, staying connected with loved ones through video calls, and even accessing productivity tools to help with day-to-day tasks. Don't worry if some of these terms sound unfamiliar now; each topic will be explained in clear, relatable language, with plenty of examples and practical tips.

One of the best parts about this guide is that it's designed for flexibility. If you're curious about a specific feature, you can jump to that section without feeling like you're missing something. On the other hand, if you prefer a more step-by-step approach, you're welcome to read from cover to cover. Every part of the book builds on what came before, so you'll always feel supported as you progress.

The aim is for you to finish each chapter feeling like you've truly understood what you've read and can confidently apply what you've learned.

This book also includes troubleshooting tips to help you solve common issues on your own. Technology can sometimes be unpredictable, and knowing how to handle minor challenges, like a Wi-Fi connection issue or an app that won't open, can make a big difference. These troubleshooting sections aren't there to make things more complicated; they're intended to empower you to feel capable and independent, even when things don't go exactly as planned. By the time you reach the end of this book, you'll have a solid understanding of your MacBook's features, and you'll be equipped with skills that make everyday tasks smoother and more enjoyable.

As you move through this guide, remember that it's okay to take breaks, revisit sections, and learn at a pace that feels right for you.

Some readers might find certain topics easier than others, and that's perfectly fine. The goal isn't to rush but to make the learning process enjoyable and rewarding. By giving yourself time to practice, repeat, and explore, you'll gradually find yourself becoming more comfortable with each new feature. Every chapter is a small step toward gaining confidence, and with each page, you'll see that technology can actually be an accessible and helpful part of your daily life.

So let's begin this journey together. Your MacBook is a tool meant to simplify and enhance your daily experiences, and this guide will show you how to make the most of it, from the very basics to the more advanced features. You don't have to be a tech expert to enjoy the benefits of a MacBook, and you're not alone in figuring it all out. Let's start this adventure with an open mind and the understanding that, with a little patience, you'll soon be navigating your device with ease and confidence.

Enjoy the journey, take it one step at a time, and soon you'll see just how much you're capable of. Welcome to the world of MacBook, where learning is relaxed, the pace is yours, and each new skill is a step toward something empowering.

Chapter 1: Getting Started with Your MacBook

When you first open your MacBook box, there's a sense of excitement that comes with unwrapping a new piece of technology. This chapter will guide you through the initial steps, from unboxing to setting up your MacBook and navigating its essential features. By the end of this chapter, you'll feel comfortable with the basics and ready to dive into the more advanced aspects of your device.

1.1 Unboxing and Initial Setup

Inside the box, you'll find your MacBook along with a few key accessories. Apple keeps things simple and streamlined, so you'll likely see the MacBook itself, a USB-C charging cable, and a power adapter for plugging into an outlet.

If you've purchased a MacBook with Touch ID (a fingerprint sensor) or FaceTime HD camera, those features are built into the device, meaning no extra setup or parts are needed. Take a moment to check these items and make sure everything looks ready to go.

Now that you have your MacBook and accessories, it's time to set it up. Start by plugging in the USB-C charging cable to both your MacBook and the power adapter, then connect it to a wall outlet. You'll see the MacBook's screen come to life once it starts receiving power. The initial setup is straightforward but important, as this is where you'll configure the fundamental settings and features you'll use every day. When you open your MacBook, press the power button on the upper right side of the keyboard.

You'll see the Apple logo as your device starts up, and from here, you'll be guided through a series of steps to personalize your MacBook's settings.

Let's go over some physical features you'll need to understand to use your MacBook effectively.

The power button is typically in the top right corner of the keyboard and is used to turn your MacBook on or off. The trackpad, located just below the keyboard, is your main way of controlling the cursor, much like a mouse on a desktop computer. You can move the cursor by sliding your finger across the trackpad, and you can click by pressing down on it. The MacBook's keyboard is similar to a standard keyboard, but Apple has added some helpful shortcuts and keys designed to make navigation more intuitive. As you explore, you'll become familiar with shortcuts like Command (⌘) and Option (⌥), which are used for various tasks throughout the macOS system.

1.2 Navigating the Setup Assistant

Once you've powered up your MacBook, you'll be greeted by the Setup Assistant, a step-by-step guide designed to help you configure your device for the first time.

The Setup Assistant will walk you through essential settings, beginning with language and region options. Start by choosing the language you're most comfortable with, as this will apply to the entire system, including menus, commands, and notifications. You'll then be prompted to select your region or country, which will set up location-based preferences such as time zone and regional formats for dates, numbers, and currencies.

Next, you'll connect your MacBook to Wi-Fi. You'll see a list of available networks, so select your home Wi-Fi network, enter the password if prompted, and confirm the connection. Once you're connected, your MacBook will have access to the internet, which will be essential for downloading updates, using online services, and setting up your Apple ID.

If you don't have your Wi-Fi password handy, you can skip this step and connect to Wi-Fi later through the system settings.

After Wi-Fi, you'll be prompted to sign in with your Apple ID or create one if you don't have it yet. The Apple ID is your personal account that allows you to access Apple's services, including the App Store, iCloud, and iMessage. If you already have an Apple ID from another Apple device, you can use the same account here. If not, follow the on-screen instructions to set up a new Apple ID, which typically involves providing an email address, creating a secure password, and answering a few security questions. This step also lets you enable iCloud, Apple's cloud storage service, which is useful for backing up files, syncing data across Apple devices, and sharing files with others.

The Setup Assistant will then guide you through privacy settings, giving you control over the data you choose to share with Apple.

For example, you can decide whether to enable location services, which lets your MacBook know your location to improve apps like Maps, Weather, and Photos. Privacy settings can feel complex, but they're important for ensuring your personal information stays secure. The Setup Assistant offers brief explanations for each setting, so feel free to adjust them based on your comfort level with sharing information.

Finally, you'll be presented with Apple's terms and conditions, a standard agreement required to use the MacBook and Apple's services. Although it's a lengthy document, it's recommended to read through it or at least review the main points. Once you agree, the Setup Assistant will complete the setup process, and you'll be ready to start exploring your MacBook's features.

1.3 Exploring the Desktop and Basic Features

With the setup complete, your MacBook will display the desktop, which is your main workspace. The desktop consists of a background (which you can customize), along with a few core elements that will become very familiar to you. One of the first things you'll notice is the Dock, located at the bottom of the screen. The Dock is a convenient bar that contains icons for your frequently used applications. You can click an icon to open the app and drag icons to rearrange them based on your preferences. The Dock can be customized to include only the apps you use regularly, making it easier to access your favorite tools.

Above the desktop is the Menu Bar, a slim bar that stretches across the top of your screen. The Menu Bar contains essential controls, such as the Apple logo on the far left, where you can access system options like sleep, restart, and shut down. Next to the Apple logo are menus specific to each app you open, with options like File, Edit, View, and more, depending on the app in use. To the right side of the Menu Bar, you'll see system icons like Wi-Fi, battery status, date and time, and Spotlight (a powerful search tool). The Menu Bar is a handy place to keep an eye on your MacBook's overall status.

One of the most essential parts of the macOS system is Finder, a file management application that lets you browse, organize, and manage your files. Finder opens automatically when you click the Finder icon in the Dock, revealing folders like Documents, Downloads, and Applications. Here, you can create new folders, drag and drop files, and perform basic tasks such as renaming or deleting items. Finder is designed to keep all of your files and folders in one convenient place, making it easy to stay organized.

Customizing your MacBook's settings can make it feel more like your own.

To access system settings, click the Apple logo in the Menu Bar and select "System Preferences."

In System Preferences, you can adjust display settings, sound volume, and trackpad preferences, among other things. For example, you can change the desktop background by selecting "Desktop & Screen Saver" and choosing from Apple's collection of images or adding one of your own photos. System Preferences offers a wide range of options to personalize your MacBook experience, so feel free to explore each category and set things up to match your preferences.

Finally, the MacBook's trackpad is an incredibly versatile tool that supports gestures, which are simple hand movements that help you navigate faster. For instance, you can swipe with two fingers to scroll through web pages, pinch to zoom in or out, or use a three-finger swipe to switch between open applications.

These gestures may take a bit of practice, but once you get the hang of them, they make navigating your MacBook feel more intuitive and efficient. By familiarizing yourself with the desktop and these basic features, you'll feel ready to explore more advanced aspects of your MacBook with confidence.

Chapter 2: Connecting to the Internet and Setting Up Accounts

The ability to connect to the internet and manage accounts is fundamental to getting the most out of your MacBook. From browsing the web to sending emails and syncing data across devices, these initial steps unlock essential features that make your MacBook a powerful tool. This chapter will guide you through connecting to Wi-Fi, setting up your email accounts, and configuring your Apple ID and iCloud for seamless integration with Apple's ecosystem.

2.1 Connecting to Wi-Fi

Connecting to Wi-Fi is one of the first things you'll want to do when setting up your MacBook, as many features depend on internet access. Start by clicking on the Wi-Fi icon in the top-right corner of your screen. This will display a list of available networks. Locate your home Wi-Fi network from the list and select it. You'll be prompted to enter the Wi-Fi password, which is typically found on your router or provided by your internet service provider. Once you've entered the password, click "Connect." Your MacBook should now be connected to the internet, and you'll see the Wi-Fi icon become fully shaded, indicating a successful connection.

In some cases, you might encounter issues when trying to connect. If you're unable to connect, the first step is to double-check that you've entered the correct password, as even a small typo can prevent the connection.

If you're certain the password is correct and the connection still isn't working, try restarting your router by unplugging it for a few seconds and plugging it back in. After the router restarts, wait a minute or two, then attempt to reconnect to Wi-Fi on your MacBook. If you're still having trouble, you may want to try connecting to another network to determine if the issue is with your MacBook or your Wi-Fi network.

Another troubleshooting step is to reset your MacBook's network settings. Go to the Apple menu in the top-left corner, select "System Preferences," then click on "Network." From here, select your Wi-Fi network, click the minus sign (-) to remove it, and then reconnect by selecting it from the list again. This refreshes the connection and can resolve minor connectivity issues. If problems persist, you may want to contact your internet service provider, as the issue could be on their end.

2.2 Setting Up Email Accounts

Once you're connected to the internet, setting up email accounts on your MacBook is the next step. Email is a primary way to communicate, and having it readily accessible on your MacBook is both convenient and practical. To start, open the Mail app, which you'll find in the Dock (the row of icons at the bottom of your screen). When you open Mail for the first time, it will prompt you to add an account. Select your email provider from the list, which typically includes popular options like iCloud, Gmail, Yahoo, and Microsoft Exchange. If your provider isn't listed, select "Other Mail Account" and follow the steps to manually add your email.

After selecting your provider, enter your email address and password, then click "Sign In." The Mail app will attempt to connect to your account, and if successful, it will automatically configure your email settings.

You'll see a confirmation once the account is successfully added, and your inbox will begin loading your recent emails. To check your email at any time, open the Mail app, and you'll see a list of folders like Inbox, Sent, and Trash. You can click on any folder to view its contents, making it easy to stay organized and manage your communications.

Once your email account is set up, try sending your first email to get a feel for how the Mail app works. Click on the "New Message" button, usually represented by an envelope icon or a pencil symbol at the top of the Mail window. In the "To" field, enter the email address of the person you wish to contact. You can also add multiple recipients by separating each address with a comma. Write your message in the text box below, and when you're ready, click "Send." Your message will be sent, and a copy will be saved in the Sent folder, allowing you to refer back to it later if needed.

The Mail app also makes it easy to manage your contacts and keep your inbox organized.

To add a contact, open an email from someone you frequently communicate with, then click on their email address to see the option to "Add to Contacts." This saves their information to your Contacts app, making it easier to find and email them in the future. Additionally, you can create folders or "mailboxes" within the Mail app to organize your emails by category. For instance, you might create folders for personal emails, work-related messages, or newsletters. Simply click "Mailbox" in the top menu, select "New Mailbox," and name the folder. This organization helps keep your inbox tidy, especially as the volume of emails grows over time.

2.3 Setting Up Apple ID and iCloud

An Apple ID is central to your experience on a MacBook, as it grants access to Apple's services like the App Store, iCloud, and FaceTime.

If you already have an Apple ID from a previous Apple device, you can use the same account.

If not, setting one up is straightforward. Go to the Apple menu, select "System Preferences," then click "Sign In" at the top of the window. Follow the prompts to create a new Apple ID by entering an email address, creating a password, and setting up security questions. This Apple ID will serve as your personal account for all Apple services, keeping your data and purchases synchronized across devices.

Once you have an Apple ID, you can set up iCloud, Apple's cloud storage and syncing service. iCloud is especially useful for backing up important data, such as photos, documents, and contacts. When iCloud is enabled, your data is securely stored on Apple's servers, allowing you to access it from any Apple device. To activate iCloud, go to System Preferences, click on "Apple ID," and then select "iCloud" from the sidebar.

Here, you'll see a list of features you can enable, including Photos, Contacts, and Calendars. Toggle on each option you'd like to sync, and iCloud will automatically back up and sync that data across your devices.

iCloud also includes a feature called iCloud Drive, which functions as a cloud-based file storage system. iCloud Drive allows you to save documents and files, making them accessible from your MacBook, iPhone, iPad, or even a Windows PC. To use iCloud Drive, open Finder and look for "iCloud Drive" in the sidebar. You can create folders, save files, and even share documents with others through this feature. iCloud Drive offers a convenient way to keep your files organized and available wherever you need them, eliminating the need for physical storage devices.

In addition to storage, iCloud provides several services that enhance your MacBook experience.

For example, iCloud Photos stores your photo library in the cloud, so you can access your pictures on all your devices. Any photo you take on your iPhone will automatically appear on your MacBook, and vice versa. Similarly, iCloud Backup regularly backs up your data, ensuring that you won't lose important information if something happens to your device. By enabling these features, you can enjoy a more integrated experience, as iCloud keeps your data secure and accessible.

Setting up and managing iCloud is simple, and Apple provides options to upgrade storage if needed. While Apple offers 5GB of free iCloud storage, you may find that this is limited if you plan to store a large number of photos or files. Upgrading to a larger plan is easy; simply go to System Preferences, select "Apple ID," then "iCloud," and choose "Manage" to view your storage options. From there, you can select a storage plan that fits your needs, with options for 50GB, 200GB, or even 2TB.

With your Apple ID and iCloud set up, your MacBook is now connected to Apple's ecosystem, allowing you to enjoy seamless integration and convenient access to all your data. The ability to sync, store, and share data through iCloud makes your MacBook more versatile, ensuring that your information is always at your fingertips, no matter which Apple device you're using.

Chapter 3: Navigating and Personalizing Your MacBook

Mastering your MacBook's navigation and personalizing it to fit your preferences can transform it from a standard device into something that truly feels like your own. In this chapter, we'll explore the Finder, which serves as the command center for organizing files and folders, as well as various ways to customize your desktop and system settings. You'll also learn how to find, install, and manage applications that enhance your productivity and enjoyment. By the end of this chapter, you'll feel confident navigating your MacBook and making adjustments to make it work best for you.

3.1 Understanding Finder and File Management

Finder is the essential tool on your MacBook for locating and managing files. Whether it's a document, photo, or application, Finder helps you organize and access everything you store on your Mac. When you open Finder, you'll see a window divided into sections, with a sidebar on the left and a main viewing area on the right. The sidebar provides quick access to common locations, like "Applications," "Documents," "Downloads," and "Desktop," while the main area displays the contents of the selected location.

Finder's main function is to help you stay organized with folders. By using folders, you can group related files together, making it easy to find what you need without having to sift through a cluttered desktop. For instance, you might create a folder for work documents, another for personal photos, and perhaps one for important receipts. To create a folder, simply right-click (or Control-click) within any Finder window and select "New Folder." Once created, you can give it a descriptive name, like "Vacation Photos" or "Financial Records," which makes it easier to remember its contents.

Renaming files or folders is equally simple. Click once on the item's name, wait a moment, then click again to make it editable. Alternatively, you can right-click and choose "Rename" from the menu. To delete a file or folder, click on it once to select it, then press the "Delete" key on your keyboard. The file will move to the Trash, where it will remain until you empty it. This system lets you safely remove files without permanently deleting them immediately, in case you change your mind.

Efficient file organization is key to a smooth experience on your MacBook.

Consider adopting a naming convention for your files, especially for important documents you'll want to access later. For example, you might use dates in the format "YYYY-MM-DD" for financial documents, or include project names in work files. Additionally, you can use color tags to categorize files based on priority or type. Right-click on any file, select a color tag, and this will make the file easier to spot in Finder. By developing a consistent organization strategy, you'll save time and reduce frustration when you need to locate specific files.

3.2 Customizing the Desktop and System Preferences

Customizing your desktop is a quick and enjoyable way to make your MacBook feel more personal. Start by changing the wallpaper to something that brings you joy or makes it easier to concentrate. Right-click on the desktop and select "Change Desktop Background."

From here, you can choose from Apple's collection of beautiful wallpapers or add your own photos by selecting "Photos" from the sidebar. Pick a wallpaper that suits your style—whether it's a scenic landscape or a family photo, this small change can make your workspace feel more welcoming.

The Dock, located at the bottom of the screen, is another feature that you can customize to fit your workflow. The Dock holds icons for frequently used applications, which makes it easy to launch your favorite tools quickly. To add an app to the Dock, open it, then right-click its icon in the Dock and select "Options" followed by "Keep in Dock." You can remove apps by right-clicking and choosing "Remove from Dock." You can also reposition icons by dragging them to the desired spot, creating a Dock that reflects your needs and habits.

System Preferences allows you to dive deeper into customization by adjusting various settings. For instance, you can explore "Sound" settings to adjust alert volumes or set the default output device if you're using headphones or external speakers. "Display" settings let you adjust brightness, resolution, and even enable Night Shift, which reduces blue light for a warmer display during evening hours. Night Shift can be easier on your eyes and may help with sleep if you often use your MacBook before bed.

Accessibility settings within System Preferences provide options to make your MacBook more user-friendly. For instance, "Zoom" lets you magnify the screen, while "VoiceOver" reads out on-screen text. You can enable keyboard shortcuts for quick access to these features, making it easy to toggle them as needed. Additionally, you'll find settings for increasing cursor size, adjusting contrast, and enabling text-to-speech options.

These tools are especially helpful if you have specific accessibility needs, and they ensure you can navigate your MacBook comfortably.

System Preferences also includes options to adjust energy settings, which affect your MacBook's battery life. In the "Energy Saver" section, you can set your MacBook to go to sleep after a certain period of inactivity or dim the display when running on battery power. Small adjustments like these can extend your battery life, making your MacBook more efficient when you're on the go.

3.3 Installing and Managing Applications

Applications, or "apps," are programs that allow you to perform specific tasks on your MacBook. Whether it's checking the weather, managing your calendar, or editing photos, there's likely an app for everything you need.

The App Store, pre-installed on your MacBook, is the easiest and safest way to find new applications. Open the App Store by clicking its icon in the Dock, then use the search bar to find specific apps or browse through categories like "Productivity" or "Entertainment." When you find an app you want, click "Get" or the price button, then follow the prompts to install it.

In addition to the App Store, you may encounter third-party applications, which are apps not distributed through Apple's official store. These apps can be downloaded from websites but require extra caution, as not all third-party software is safe. Before downloading, ensure that the source is trustworthy and reputable. When you install a third-party app, macOS may warn you that it's from an unidentified developer. If you're confident in the app's safety, you can allow it by going to System Preferences, selecting

"Security & Privacy," and clicking "Open Anyway" next to the app's name.

Managing your applications is essential for keeping your MacBook organized and ensuring that you only have the tools you truly need. Over time, you may find that you've accumulated several apps you rarely use. To uninstall an app, open Finder, go to the "Applications" folder, and drag the app's icon to the Trash. This method works for most applications, but some apps may come with their own uninstaller, which you can use by following the instructions provided by the developer.

The Launchpad, accessible through the Dock, is another way to view and organize your apps. Launchpad displays all installed applications in a grid layout, similar to the home screen on an iPhone. You can rearrange apps by dragging them to different positions or even create folders by dragging one app on top of another.

This setup is especially useful if you like having quick access to all your apps in one place. Launchpad can be customized to display only the apps you frequently use, making it easier to find what you need at a glance.

Keeping your apps updated is also crucial, as updates often include new features, bug fixes, and security improvements. To check for updates, open the App Store, click on the "Updates" tab, and follow the prompts to install available updates. For third-party applications, you'll typically see an "Update" option within the app itself or receive notifications when a new version is available. Regularly updating your apps helps ensure that you're using the latest, most secure versions.

By understanding Finder, customizing your MacBook's desktop, and managing your applications, you'll be able to create a workspace that reflects your unique preferences and needs.

This level of control not only makes your MacBook more enjoyable to use but also enhances your efficiency, allowing you to navigate, organize, and personalize your device with ease.

Chapter 4: Communication and Staying Connected

Staying in touch with family, friends, and colleagues has never been easier, thanks to the various communication tools available on your MacBook. From FaceTime for video calls to the Messages app for quick chats and even social media for broader connections, your MacBook has everything you need to stay connected. This chapter will guide you through setting up and using FaceTime and Messages, as well as safely accessing and managing popular social media platforms. With these tools at your fingertips, you'll find that reaching out to others is simple and enjoyable.

4.1 FaceTime and Video Calls

FaceTime is Apple's built-in app for making video and audio calls, which is especially useful for staying in touch with loved ones, no matter where they are. Setting up FaceTime is a straightforward process, and once it's ready, you can make calls to anyone with an Apple device. To get started, open the FaceTime app, which you'll find in the Dock or by searching in Spotlight. The first time you open FaceTime, you may be prompted to sign in with your Apple ID. If you're already signed in on your MacBook, FaceTime will automatically connect to your account. If not, enter your Apple ID and password to complete the setup.

Once FaceTime is set up, making video or audio calls is easy. To initiate a call, open the FaceTime app and enter the email address or phone number of the person you want to reach. If the contact is saved in your Contacts app, you can simply type their name, and FaceTime will pull up their information. Click on the "Video" button for a video call or the "Audio" button for an audio-only call. FaceTime will ring the recipient, and once they answer, you'll be connected. You'll see their face on the screen (or hear their voice if it's an audio call), and they'll see or hear you as well. During a video call, you can adjust the volume, switch between front and back cameras (if using an iPhone or iPad), and even add filters or effects for a bit of fun.

Sometimes, FaceTime calls may encounter issues, such as poor video quality or trouble connecting. If this happens, check your internet connection first, as a strong Wi-Fi signal is essential for smooth video calls. You may also want to restart FaceTime by closing and reopening the app. If the problem persists, try signing out of FaceTime and then signing back in by going to the "FaceTime" menu at the top left of the screen, selecting "Preferences," and clicking "Sign Out." Signing back in refreshes the connection and often resolves minor issues. If you continue to have trouble, ensure that your MacBook's operating system is up to date, as updates often include bug fixes and performance improvements for FaceTime.

4.2 Messages and Communication Apps

The Messages app on your MacBook is another powerful tool for staying connected, allowing you to send texts, photos, videos, and more. Messages is compatible with both iMessage (Apple's messaging service) and SMS, meaning you can message anyone, whether they're using an Apple device or not. To get started, open the Messages app, which you'll find in the Dock or Applications folder. The first time you open it, you'll be prompted to sign in with your Apple ID if you haven't already. Signing in with your Apple ID enables iMessage, so you can send messages to other Apple users without incurring any SMS fees.

To send a message, click on the "New Message" icon, which looks like a pencil and paper.

In the "To" field, type the name, email address, or phone number of the person you want to contact. If they're an Apple user, the text bubble will appear in blue, indicating an iMessage; if not, it will appear in green, indicating SMS. Type your message in the text field at the bottom of the window, and press "Enter" or "Return" to send it. You can also send photos, videos, and other attachments by clicking on the camera icon next to the text field, selecting the file you want, and hitting "Send." This makes it easy to share memories, documents, or quick photos.

Messages on Mac also supports fun extras like stickers, emojis, and special effects. To add an emoji, click on the smiley face icon within the text field and select the emoji you want. Stickers are available through downloadable packs from the App Store and can add a playful touch to your conversations.

You can also send message effects, such as balloons or confetti, by typing your message, right-clicking on the send button, and selecting an effect. These little features make messaging more engaging and add a personal touch to your conversations.

Managing your Messages settings can help keep your chats organized. Go to the "Messages" menu at the top left of your screen, select "Preferences," and customize your notifications, which control how you're alerted to new messages. You can also adjust your account settings here, like choosing whether your MacBook should sync messages from your other Apple devices. To organize conversations, you can pin important contacts to the top of your message list by right-clicking on their conversation and selecting "Pin." This keeps your frequent contacts easily accessible, so you don't have to scroll through old conversations to find them.

4.3 Setting Up and Using Social Media

Social media platforms like Facebook, Instagram, and Twitter allow you to stay connected with a larger community, share updates, and view content from family, friends, and other people you follow. Accessing social media on your MacBook is as easy as visiting the platform's website in Safari or another web browser, or by downloading the desktop app if available. Once you're on the site, log in with your username and password, and you'll be able to access your feed, messages, notifications, and profile.

If you're new to social media, it's worth starting with one platform, like Facebook, where you can connect with people you know, share photos, and join groups based on your interests. Facebook has a simple setup process; after creating an account, you'll be guided through steps to add a profile picture, provide some basic information, and connect with friends. Instagram, another popular platform, focuses on photo and video sharing and is a great option if you enjoy visual content. Twitter, on the other hand, allows you to follow news, opinions, and quick updates from a wide range of users.

Staying safe on social media is important, especially given privacy concerns. Start by reviewing the privacy settings on each platform to control who can see your posts, contact you, or tag you in photos. For example, on Facebook, you can adjust who sees your profile information and posts by going to "Settings & Privacy" and selecting "Privacy Checkup." It's a good idea to limit your posts to friends only, rather than making them public, to keep your information more secure.

Be cautious about accepting friend requests from strangers, as some profiles may be fake. Similarly, avoid clicking on suspicious links, even if they come from people you know, as these can sometimes lead to scams or phishing attempts.

Managing notifications on social media can help you avoid feeling overwhelmed by alerts. Each platform offers settings to customize which notifications you receive and how they're delivered. For instance, Facebook allows you to choose between email, push notifications, or in-app alerts for activities like friend requests, comments, and group updates. You can adjust these in the "Settings & Privacy" section under "Notifications." If you find that notifications are interrupting your day, consider limiting them to essential updates or setting specific times to check your social media.

With FaceTime, Messages, and social media at your fingertips, your MacBook becomes a hub for connecting with people near and far. These tools not only make communication easy and accessible but also open up new ways to share experiences and stay informed.

By exploring these features and adjusting your settings, you'll find a balance that allows you to stay connected without feeling overwhelmed.

Chapter 5: Productivity and Everyday Apps

Your MacBook isn't just a device for staying connected—it's also an incredible tool for getting organized, managing daily tasks, and staying productive. With built-in apps like Safari, Calendar, Reminders, and Notes, your MacBook has everything you need to keep track of important information, plan your schedule, and capture ideas. In this chapter, we'll explore these core apps, walking you through how to use them effectively and customize them to fit your lifestyle. By the end of this chapter, you'll be equipped with practical skills to make everyday tasks easier and more organized.

5.1 Using Safari for Browsing the Web

Safari is Apple's default web browser and an excellent tool for browsing the internet on your MacBook. It's designed to be fast, secure, and user-friendly, making it an ideal choice whether you're reading the news, shopping online, or doing research. When you open Safari, you'll see a search bar at the top where you can type in the website URL or search terms. Safari will take you to your destination or display search results instantly.

Tabs in Safari allow you to have multiple pages open simultaneously, making it easy to switch between websites. To open a new tab, click the "+" button next to your current tab, or use the keyboard shortcut Command + T. This feature is helpful if you want to keep several websites open at once, such as an article, an email inbox, and a shopping site.

You can switch between tabs by clicking on them at the top of the window, or close them by clicking the "x" on each tab.

Safari also includes a bookmarking feature to save websites you frequently visit. To bookmark a page, go to the top menu, select "Bookmarks," then "Add Bookmark." You can organize bookmarks into folders for easy access, which is handy if you have a list of favorite sites you visit regularly. The History feature is another useful tool, as it keeps a record of recently visited sites. To access your browsing history, click "History" in the top menu, where you'll see a list of sites in chronological order. This is helpful if you accidentally close a tab or need to revisit a page from a previous session.

Browsing safely is essential, and Safari includes several tools to protect your privacy. Be cautious about visiting unfamiliar websites, especially those with excessive pop-ups or suspicious ads.

Safari's built-in pop-up blocker helps by stopping most unwanted windows from appearing. If you encounter a website that seems suspicious, it's best to exit immediately to avoid potential scams. Safari also warns you if a site is known to be unsafe, helping you avoid phishing scams and malicious content.

Safari allows you to enhance your browsing experience with extensions, which are small add-ons that expand the browser's functionality. To install extensions, go to the App Store, search for Safari extensions, and download the ones you find useful. For example, you might install an ad blocker to remove intrusive ads or a password manager to keep track of your login credentials securely. Another useful feature in Safari is Reader Mode, which simplifies web pages by removing ads and distractions, leaving only the text and main images.

To activate Reader Mode, click the "Reader" icon on the left side of the search bar while on a compatible page. This is great for focused reading, especially on news or blog sites.

5.2 Staying Organized with Calendar and Reminders

The Calendar app on your MacBook is designed to help you keep track of events, appointments, and important dates. When you open Calendar, you'll see a monthly view by default, with each day divided into hourly segments. To add a new event, double-click on the desired date, or click the "+" button in the toolbar. A window will appear where you can enter details like the event's name, time, location, and any additional notes. You can set the event to repeat (such as weekly or monthly) and even invite others if it's a group meeting.

In addition to Calendar, the Reminders app is useful for managing tasks that don't necessarily have a specific time but still need to be completed.

Open the Reminders app, click "New Reminder," and type in the task. You can set due dates, assign priorities, and even add notes to each reminder. If you'd like to be reminded at a particular time or place, use the "i" button next to each reminder to customize alert settings. This feature is perfect for things like grocery lists, errands, or project deadlines.

One of the best aspects of Calendar and Reminders is that they can sync across your Apple devices. If you enter an event or reminder on your MacBook, it will automatically appear on your iPhone or iPad if you're signed in with the same Apple ID. This ensures that your schedule and to-do list are always up-to-date, no matter which device you're using. To enable syncing, go to System Preferences on your MacBook, select "Apple ID," then "iCloud," and ensure that Calendar and Reminders are checked.

Managing notifications is key to staying on top of events without being overwhelmed by alerts.

In Calendar, you can set up reminders for each event, with options like "5 minutes before" or "1 day before" the event.

Reminders app notifications work similarly, allowing you to receive alerts at specific times or locations. Go to "System Preferences," select "Notifications," then adjust settings for Calendar and Reminders. Here, you can choose alert sounds, the style of notification, and whether you'd like a notification banner or alert that stays on your screen until dismissed.

5.3 Taking Notes and Staying Organized

The Notes app is an incredibly versatile tool on your MacBook, perfect for jotting down ideas, organizing lists, or keeping track of important information. Open Notes, and you'll see a sidebar on the left where you can view existing notes and folders. To create a new note, click on the "New Note "icon at the top of the window.

A blank note will appear where you can type text, add formatting, or create lists. Notes automatically save your work as you type, so there's no need to worry about losing information.

One of the strengths of the Notes app is its formatting options, which make it easy to organize content within a note. You can add titles, headings, bulleted lists, or checklists to keep everything structured. For example, if you're planning a trip, you might create a checklist of items to pack, or if you're working on a project, you can organize notes by topic or priority. To format text, select the portion you'd like to modify, then use the formatting toolbar at the top of the note to apply the desired style.

Notes also allows you to add media, which is helpful for creating richer, more detailed entries. You can drag and drop images directly into a note, making it ideal for storing visual references like photos, charts, or diagrams.

You can also add links to websites by pasting them into a note, which is useful for research or saving articles you'd like to read later. Additionally, you can attach checklists, which is great for task management. Just type out the list, highlight it, and select the checklist option from the toolbar. This creates checkable boxes, allowing you to mark items as complete.

Organizing your notes is simple with folders. To create a new folder, click on the "New Folder" button at the bottom of the sidebar, name it, and start adding relevant notes. This is particularly helpful if you have a lot of notes and want to group them by category, like "Work," "Personal," or "Travel." You can also use tags within notes to make them searchable; just type "#" followed by a keyword, and Notes will recognize it as a tag. Tags make it easier to find related notes, even if they're in different folders.

Notes can also be shared with others, making it a useful tool for collaboration.

To share a note, open it, click the "Share" button at the top, and select the person you want to share it with. They'll receive an invitation to view or edit the note, depending on the permissions you set. This feature is great for family planning, team projects, or group events, as it allows everyone to contribute and stay informed.

With Safari, Calendar, Reminders, and Notes, your MacBook provides all the tools you need to stay productive and organized. By using these apps to their fullest, you can streamline your daily tasks, keep track of important dates, and ensure you have all the information you need at your fingertips. With a bit of practice, these tools will become second nature, making your MacBook an invaluable companion in both personal and professional life.

Chapter 6: Advanced MacBook Features

As you grow comfortable with the basic functions of your MacBook, you may want to explore some of its more advanced features. These tools not only enhance productivity but also provide convenience, security, and personalization that can make your experience with the device feel truly seamless. In this chapter, we'll delve into using Siri as your virtual assistant, managing files and data through iCloud, and fine-tuning your MacBook's security and privacy settings. By the end of this chapter, you'll have a deeper understanding of your MacBook's capabilities and how to tailor them to your needs.

6.1 Introduction to Siri

Siri, Apple's voice-activated assistant, is designed to make tasks on your MacBook easier, from setting reminders to answering questions. To set up Siri, go to the Apple menu in the top-left corner, select "System Preferences," then click on "Siri." Here, you'll find options to enable Siri, choose a voice, and set your preferred language. For hands-free access, you can enable the "Listen for 'Hey Siri'" option, allowing you to activate Siri simply by speaking. This feature is especially convenient when your hands are busy or when you want to perform tasks quickly without typing.

Once Siri is set up, you can start using it by saying "Hey Siri" (if you've enabled voice activation) or by clicking the Siri icon in the top-right corner of your screen. Siri can help you with a wide range of tasks.

For example, you can ask Siri to check the weather, set reminders, send messages, or look up information online.

Siri is particularly useful for multitasking; if you're working on a document, you can ask Siri to open a specific app, play music, or read out an email, all without interrupting your workflow. To maximize Siri's effectiveness, try being specific with your requests. Instead of saying "Remind me," you might say, "Remind me to call John at 3 PM tomorrow." The more detailed you are, the better Siri can assist you.

Siri also integrates with many MacBook features, allowing you to make quick adjustments without navigating through menus. For instance, you can ask Siri to "Turn on Do Not Disturb," or "Increase the screen brightness." Siri can even search within your files by saying things like "Show me files from last week" or "Find my recent documents."

This makes Siri a helpful tool for accessing information quickly, especially when you're working with large amounts of data or files.

To make Siri more useful, consider personalizing the way you use it. Siri learns from your interactions, so the more you use it, the better it will understand your preferences. You can also teach Siri pronunciation for contacts with unusual names, or link Siri to specific apps to extend its functionality. By tailoring Siri's settings and interactions, you'll find that it becomes an even more intuitive and efficient assistant.

6.2 iCloud and File Sharing

iCloud is Apple's cloud storage service, which lets you store, access, and share files across all your Apple devices. When you activate iCloud on your MacBook, you can save photos, documents, and other files to the cloud, freeing up local storage and ensuring your data is backed up securely.

To set up iCloud, go to "System Preferences," click on "Apple ID," and select "iCloud." Here, you can choose which apps and data to sync with iCloud, such as Photos, Contacts, Calendars, and Safari. Once enabled, iCloud will automatically keep this data updated across all devices signed in with the same Apple ID.

One of the core features of iCloud is iCloud Drive, a virtual storage space where you can save files and access them from any device. To open iCloud Drive, go to Finder, where you'll see it listed in the sidebar. You can create folders, drag and drop files, and organize your documents just as you would on your MacBook's internal storage. iCloud Drive is especially useful for accessing files remotely.

For example, if you save a presentation on your MacBook and later need to access it on your iPhone, iCloud Drive makes it seamless to do so.

iCloud also facilitates collaboration, allowing you to share files and folders with friends, family, or colleagues. To share a file, right-click on it in iCloud Drive, select "Share," and choose your preferred sharing method, like email or message. You can control the level of access, deciding whether others can only view the file or make edits as well. This feature is helpful for group projects or for sharing files like photos or documents with family members.

Managing your iCloud storage is straightforward. Apple offers 5GB of free iCloud storage, but you may find that you need more space if you plan to store a large number of photos, videos, or files. To view your iCloud storage, go to "System Preferences," select "Apple ID," and then click "Manage" next to iCloud. Here, you can see a breakdown of how your storage is being used and consider upgrading to a larger plan if needed.

Apple offers affordable options for additional storage, with plans ranging from 50GB to 2TB.

6.3 Security and Privacy Features

Keeping your MacBook secure and your data private is a priority, and macOS offers a variety of tools to help you achieve this. One of the most convenient security features is Touch ID, available on certain MacBook models. Touch ID allows you to unlock your MacBook, make purchases, and sign in to apps with a fingerprint. To set up Touch ID, go to "System Preferences," select "Touch ID," and follow the instructions to add your fingerprint. This feature not only adds an extra layer of security but also makes it quicker and easier to unlock your device.

Beyond Touch ID, macOS includes extensive privacy settings to help protect your personal information. To access these, go to "System Preferences" and click on "Security & Privacy."

Here, you'll find four tabs: General, FileVault, Firewall, and Privacy. The General tab lets you set a password for your MacBook and adjust security options, such as requiring a password immediately after sleep or screen saver begins. FileVault, found under the FileVault tab, is a feature that encrypts your entire hard drive, protecting your data from unauthorized access. Turning on FileVault is a good idea if you store sensitive information on your MacBook.

The Firewall tab allows you to enable a firewall, which blocks unwanted incoming network connections, adding another layer of protection. Enabling the firewall can be especially useful if you're using your MacBook on public Wi-Fi networks, as it helps to keep out potential threats. Finally, the Privacy tab lets you control which apps have access to your location, contacts, camera, microphone, and other sensitive data.

By reviewing these settings, you can make sure that only trusted apps have permission to access your information.

Screen Time is another helpful tool, especially if you want to monitor and limit the amount of time spent on your MacBook. Screen Time, found in System Preferences, tracks your activity and provides a report showing which apps and websites you use most frequently. This feature can be useful for managing productivity, as it helps you see where you might be spending too much time. You can set daily limits for specific apps, schedule downtime, and even block certain websites. Screen Time also includes parental control features, which allow you to restrict access to certain content if younger users are using your MacBook.

Parental Controls within Screen Time provide additional customization for families. You can set restrictions on app usage, block inappropriate websites, and control access to purchases and downloads. To set up Parental Controls, open Screen Time in System Preferences and select the child's profile or device. Here, you can choose settings that limit access based on age-appropriate guidelines, helping to ensure a safe online experience for younger users.

By using Siri, iCloud, and the security features available on your MacBook, you'll be able to unlock powerful tools that enhance productivity and safeguard your data. These advanced features provide a level of convenience, organization, and peace of mind, allowing you to get more from your MacBook with confidence. Whether it's making quick adjustments with Siri, sharing files through iCloud, or setting up security measures, these tools give you control over your device, making it a truly personal and secure digital companion.

Chapter 7: Troubleshooting and Maintenance

Even the most reliable devices can occasionally experience issues, and your MacBook is no exception. Fortunately, many common problems have straightforward solutions, and performing regular maintenance can help keep your MacBook running smoothly. In this chapter, we'll cover troubleshooting for connectivity issues, app crashes, and slow performance. We'll also go over some regular maintenance tips, such as managing software updates, cleaning up storage, and conserving battery life. Lastly, we'll discuss where to find additional support if you encounter problems that require extra assistance.

7.1 Common Issues and Solutions

Everyday use can sometimes lead to minor issues with Wi-Fi, Bluetooth, app stability, or overall speed. Knowing how to troubleshoot these problems can save you time and frustration.

If you encounter connectivity issues, start by checking your Wi-Fi connection. Make sure you're connected to the correct network by clicking the Wi-Fi icon in the top-right corner of your screen. If the network connection seems weak or drops frequently, try restarting your router by unplugging it, waiting a minute, and then plugging it back in. On your MacBook, you can also try turning Wi-Fi off and on again from the Wi-Fi menu. If the issue persists, go to "System Preferences," select "Network," and choose "Wi-Fi."

Here, click on "Advanced," remove the network by clicking the minus sign (-), and reconnect to it by selecting it from the list and entering the password. For Bluetooth connectivity issues, go to "System Preferences," select "Bluetooth," and make sure Bluetooth is enabled. If a Bluetooth device isn't connecting, try removing it from the device list and reconnecting. Restarting your MacBook can also resolve minor connectivity issues for both Wi-Fi and Bluetooth.

Sometimes, you may notice an app crashing or freezing. If this happens, first try force-quitting the app by pressing Command + Option + Escape, selecting the unresponsive app from the list, and clicking "Force Quit." Then, reopen the app to see if it runs smoothly. If the problem persists, consider restarting your MacBook, as a fresh start can often resolve temporary glitches. Another option is to check for app updates by visiting the App Store, as developers frequently release updates to improve stability and performance.

If an app continues to crash, try uninstalling and reinstalling it.

Slow performance is another issue that can affect MacBook users, particularly if the device is older or has a lot of apps and files stored on it.

To improve speed, start by closing unnecessary apps, as having too many programs open at once can slow down performance. You can also check your storage by going to "About This Mac" under the Apple menu and selecting "Storage." Here, you'll see how much space is used and what's taking up the most room. Clearing out large, unused files or moving them to an external drive can help free up space and improve performance. In addition, restarting your MacBook periodically and keeping your software updated can prevent slowdown over time.

7.2 Regular Maintenance Tips

Routine maintenance is key to keeping your MacBook performing at its best. One of the simplest yet most effective maintenance practices is regularly updating macOS. Apple releases software updates to improve security, add new features, and fix bugs. To check for updates, go to the Apple menu, select "System Preferences," and click "Software Update." If an update is available, follow the prompts to install it. It's a good idea to enable automatic updates so your MacBook always has the latest improvements without needing to remember to update manually.

Managing storage is another crucial aspect of maintenance. Over time, files, photos, and apps can pile up, taking up valuable space on your hard drive and potentially slowing down performance. To manage your storage, go to the Apple menu, select "About This Mac," and click "Storage." Here, you'll see a breakdown of your storage usage, including categories like "Documents," "Photos," "Apps," and "System."

Consider deleting files you no longer need, moving large files to an external drive, or using iCloud to store files in the cloud rather than on your MacBook. Additionally, the "Manage" button in the Storage section offers recommendations for freeing up space, such as removing old files, emptying the Trash, or deleting unused apps.

Battery maintenance is also important, especially if you use your MacBook on the go. To maximize battery life, make a habit of adjusting your settings for energy efficiency. Go to "System Preferences," select "Energy Saver," and adjust settings like screen brightness, sleep timers, and battery percentage display. Keeping your screen brightness at a moderate level and closing unused apps can help extend battery life. Apple also recommends not leaving your MacBook plugged in at all times; instead, let the battery drain occasionally before recharging. If your battery life seems to have decreased significantly, consider visiting an Apple Store to check its health, as batteries naturally wear over time.

7.3 Finding Additional Support

Despite your best efforts, some issues may require additional support. Apple offers multiple ways to help you resolve complex problems, from online resources to in-person support at the Apple Store.

One of the best places to start is the Apple Support website (support.apple.com), where you'll find articles, videos, and step-by-step guides for common issues. The site covers a wide range of topics, from basic troubleshooting to advanced solutions, and is an excellent resource if you prefer to solve problems independently. Apple also offers a support app that you can download on your iPhone or iPad, which provides instant access to troubleshooting resources, guides, and the option to chat with Apple Support if needed.

Online forums like the Apple Support Community can also be helpful, as other MacBook users often share their experiences and solutions. You can search for topics related to your issue or ask a question in the community if you're unable to find an answer. Sometimes, seeing how other users have resolved similar problems can provide insights and solutions you may not have considered.

If you prefer in-person assistance or if the issue seems too complex to handle on your own, visiting an Apple Store is a great option. Apple's "Genius Bar" offers one-on-one technical support for hardware and software issues. To schedule an appointment, visit Apple's website or use the Apple Support app. Explain your problem when booking so the technician knows what to expect, and remember to bring your MacBook and any accessories you may need, like the power adapter. Visiting the Genius Bar can be particularly useful for issues that may require a repair or replacement of parts.

By understanding how to troubleshoot common issues, perform regular maintenance, and access additional support when needed, you'll ensure that your MacBook remains reliable and efficient. These practices help extend the lifespan of your device, allowing you to get the most out of your investment and enjoy a smooth, hassle-free experience.

Chapter 8: Tips and Tricks for Daily Use

Your MacBook is filled with tools and features designed to make everyday tasks faster, easier, and more enjoyable. From time-saving shortcuts to accessibility options that cater to different needs, learning a few of these tips can greatly enhance your user experience. This chapter will explore useful keyboard shortcuts, ways to optimize your workspace with multiple desktops, and tricks for customizing the Dock. We'll also cover accessibility features that make using your MacBook more comfortable, and finally, we'll go over how to manage notifications and alerts to keep distractions to a minimum.

8.1 Time-Saving Tips

Mastering a few keyboard shortcuts can significantly speed up how you navigate and perform tasks on your MacBook. Keyboard shortcuts allow you to accomplish common actions without reaching for your mouse or trackpad, saving seconds that add up over time. Here are some of the most useful shortcuts:

- **Command + C**: Copy selected text or items.
- **Command + V**: Paste copied text or items.
- **Command + X**: Cut selected text or items.
- **Command + Z**: Undo the last action.
- **Command + Tab**: Switch between open applications.
- **Command + Space**: Open Spotlight for quick searches.
- **Command + Shift + 4**: Take a screenshot of a selected area.

These shortcuts are only a starting point, and as you become more comfortable, you'll find others that streamline your workflow.

Another useful feature on your MacBook is **Multiple Desktops** (also called Mission Control), which allows you to create separate workspaces for different tasks. This can be especially helpful if you often switch between different projects or types of work. To access Multiple Desktops, swipe up with three fingers on the trackpad or press **Ctrl + Up Arrow**. You'll see an overview of all open windows, and at the top, an option to add a new desktop by clicking the + button.

You can then move between desktops by swiping left or right with three fingers, or by selecting the desktop you want from Mission Control. This feature keeps your work organized, so you can dedicate one desktop to emails, another to documents, and another to web browsing.

The **Split View** feature allows you to view two apps side by side, making it easy to multitask without switching between windows.

To activate Split View, click and hold the green maximize button on the top left corner of an app's window. This will allow you to drag the app to either the left or right side of the screen. Once one app is in place, select another app for the opposite side. Split View is particularly useful for tasks like copying information from a webpage into a document or watching a video while taking notes.

Customizing the **Dock** is another way to improve efficiency. The Dock holds shortcuts to your most-used apps, so adding and arranging them according to your workflow makes accessing these apps quicker. To add an app to the Dock, drag its icon from the Applications folder into the Dock. To remove an app, drag it out of the Dock until you see "Remove" appear.

You can also resize the Dock and set it to hide automatically by going to **System Preferences > Dock & Menu Bar**. Adjusting these settings creates a cleaner desktop view while still keeping essential apps at your fingertips.

8.2 Accessibility Features

Your MacBook includes a variety of **accessibility features** designed to make using the device more comfortable for everyone, including those with specific needs. One of the most popular tools is **Zoom**, which lets you magnify part of the screen to see details more clearly. To enable Zoom, go to **System Preferences > Accessibility > Zoom** and check the box to enable it. You can choose to zoom in on the entire screen or just a section. To activate Zoom, press **Option + Command + 8** and use the scroll gesture on your trackpad or mouse to adjust the zoom level.

Magnifier tools are also available, allowing you to enlarge text and images without zooming the entire screen. For example, when browsing in Safari, you can increase the text size on webpages by pressing **Command + Plus (+)** or reduce it with **Command + Minus (-)**. This is a quick and convenient way to make content easier to read without permanently adjusting your display settings.

Text-to-Speech is another helpful accessibility feature, allowing your MacBook to read selected text out loud. To enable this, go to **System Preferences > Accessibility > Spoken Content** and check the box for "Speak selected text when the key is pressed." You can then select text anywhere on your MacBook, press the assigned key, and your MacBook will read the text to you. This is a useful tool for proofreading, understanding complex information, or giving your eyes a break from reading.

If you prefer to type with your voice, **Dictation** is a feature that converts spoken words into text. To enable Dictation, go to **System Preferences > Keyboard > Dictation** and turn it on. Press the **Fn** (Function) key twice to start dictation, then begin speaking. Dictation will automatically type out your words, which can be helpful for drafting emails, notes, or documents quickly.

Your MacBook also offers **Color and Display Adjustments** to make the screen more comfortable to view. If you're sensitive to brightness, go to **System Preferences > Accessibility > Display** and adjust options like "Reduce Transparency" and "Increase Contrast." These adjustments make on-screen elements more distinct and easier to see. You can also enable "Invert Colors" if you prefer a high-contrast view or "Night Shift" to reduce blue light, which can help prevent eye strain during evening use.

8.3 Customizing Notifications and Alerts

Managing notifications on your MacBook is essential for staying focused, especially when working on important tasks. Notifications can be customized for individual apps, allowing you to prioritize which alerts you see. Go to **System Preferences > Notifications** to view a list of apps with notification permissions. Select an app, and you'll see options to enable or disable notifications, choose a sound alert, and set notification style (banners or alerts). Turning off notifications for less important apps can reduce distractions, while keeping them on for essential apps ensures you don't miss important updates.

If you need uninterrupted focus, **Do Not Disturb** mode is a valuable tool. When activated, Do Not Disturb silences notifications and hides alerts. To enable it, open the Control Center from the top-right corner of your screen and click "Do Not Disturb."

You can set it to activate for a specific time frame, like an hour or until the end of the day. For more control, go to **System Preferences > Notifications & Focus** and customize Do Not Disturb settings, such as allowing calls from certain contacts to break through or enabling it automatically during certain hours.

Focus modes take Do Not Disturb to the next level by creating custom notification filters based on your activity. You can create separate Focus modes for work, personal time, or relaxation, each with its own settings. For example, during work hours, you might only allow notifications from your calendar, email, and messaging apps. To set up Focus, go to **System Preferences > Notifications & Focus > Focus** and click "+" to add a new mode. Adjust the settings to determine which apps and contacts are allowed to send notifications in each mode.

Adjusting **volume and sound preferences** can further help you manage notifications.

Go to **System Preferences > Sound** to adjust alert volume, select a preferred sound for notifications, and control whether sounds play when certain actions are taken. Lowering the alert volume or muting sounds for non-essential notifications can help create a calmer, less distracting environment.

With these tips and tricks, you can use your MacBook more effectively and make it truly work for you. By mastering shortcuts, optimizing your workspace, using accessibility features, and managing notifications, you'll enhance productivity and make everyday tasks smoother. Your MacBook is a powerful tool, and these small adjustments ensure it adapts perfectly to your routine and needs.

Appendix

The appendix serves as a quick reference section to help you make the most of your MacBook learning experience. Here, you'll find a glossary of common terms, resources for further learning, and an index to quickly locate topics covered in the book. This section is designed to provide clarity on technical terms, direct you to helpful resources, and make it easier to revisit key information as needed.

Glossary of Common Terms

- **Apple ID**: A unique account that gives you access to Apple services, such as the App Store, iCloud, iMessage, and FaceTime.
- **Bluetooth**: A wireless technology that allows your MacBook to connect with

compatible devices, such as headphones, speakers, and keyboards.

- **Command Key (⌘)**: A key on your MacBook keyboard used in combination with other keys to create shortcuts for various actions (e.g., Command + C for copy).
- **Dock**: The bar located at the bottom of your screen that contains shortcuts to your most frequently used applications.
- **Finder**: The file management system on your MacBook that helps you organize and access files, folders, and applications.
- **Firewall**: A security feature that protects your MacBook by blocking unauthorized access to your network.
- **Force Quit**: A method to close unresponsive applications on your MacBook by pressing Command + Option + Escape and selecting the app to close.

- **iCloud**: Apple's cloud storage service, which allows you to store files, photos, and data online and access them from any Apple device.
- **iCloud Drive**: A feature within iCloud that lets you store and organize files in the cloud, accessible across all your Apple devices.
- **Mission Control**: A MacBook feature that gives you an overview of all open windows, desktops, and applications for easier multitasking.
- **Notification Center**: A panel that displays recent notifications and updates from your applications and the system.
- **Safari**: Apple's default web browser, optimized for fast and secure browsing on MacBook.
- **Siri**: Apple's voice-activated assistant that helps you perform tasks, set reminders, find information, and more through voice commands.

- **Spotlight**: A search tool on your MacBook that helps you find files, apps, documents, and information quickly by typing in keywords.
- **System Preferences**: A control panel on your MacBook that allows you to adjust settings for various features, including display, sound, notifications, and privacy.
- **Trackpad**: The touch-sensitive surface below your MacBook's keyboard that lets you control the cursor, scroll, and use gesture-based commands.
- **Touch ID**: A fingerprint recognition feature on some MacBook models that allows you to unlock your device, authorize purchases, and sign in to accounts securely.
- **Wi-Fi**: A wireless network technology that connects your MacBook to the internet without the need for cables.

Resources for Further Learning

As you continue to explore and use your MacBook, you may encounter questions or areas you'd like to learn more about. Here are some recommended resources and support options:

- **Apple Support**: Apple's official support website offers troubleshooting guides, video tutorials, and articles on a variety of topics. Visit support.apple.com to get started.
- **Apple Community Forums**: A helpful platform where Apple users discuss their experiences, share solutions, and ask questions. The community is a great place to find advice and tips from other MacBook users. Access the forums at discussions.apple.com.
- **MacMost**: A comprehensive website featuring tutorials, articles, and videos

focused on Apple products, including MacBooks. Visit macmost.com for tutorials on everything from basic functions to advanced features.

- **YouTube**: Many YouTube channels specialize in MacBook tutorials and tips. Some popular channels include "Apple Support" (Apple's official channel), "Snazzy Labs," and "9to5Mac," where you'll find step-by-step guides on MacBook-related topics.
- **MacRumors**: A website that offers news, rumors, and in-depth guides about Apple products. The "Guides" section provides detailed information on using macOS, troubleshooting, and understanding new features. Visit macrumors.com for more.
- **Lynda.com (LinkedIn Learning)**: An online learning platform with courses on using MacBooks, macOS, and productivity software. It requires a

subscription, but many public libraries offer free access.
- **Apple's Genius Bar**: For in-person support, schedule an appointment at the Genius Bar in your local Apple Store. The staff can help with hardware issues, diagnostics, and troubleshooting advice.

Index

This index provides an alphabetical list of key terms and topics covered in the book, allowing for quick and easy reference. Simply locate the term you're interested in, and turn to the corresponding page to find more information.

- Accessibility Features: Chapter 8
- Apple ID: Chapter 2, Glossary
- App Store: Chapter 3
- Battery Maintenance: Chapter 7
- Bluetooth Troubleshooting: Chapter 7
- Calendar: Chapter 5

- Color Adjustments: Chapter 8
- Command Key: Glossary
- Customizing Dock: Chapter 8
- Dictation: Chapter 8
- Do Not Disturb: Chapter 8
- FaceTime Setup: Chapter 4
- File Management: Chapter 3
- Finder Overview: Chapter 3
- Firewall: Glossary, Chapter 6
- Focus Mode: Chapter 8
- Force Quit: Glossary, Chapter 7
- iCloud: Chapter 6, Glossary
- iCloud Drive: Chapter 6, Glossary
- Keyboard Shortcuts: Chapter 8
- Magnifier: Chapter 8
- Messages: Chapter 4
- Mission Control: Glossary, Chapter 8
- Notifications: Chapter 8
- Notes: Chapter 5
- Safari: Chapter 5
- Screen Time: Chapter 6
- Security Settings: Chapter 6

- Siri Setup: Chapter 6
- Split View: Chapter 8
- Spotlight: Glossary
- Storage Management: Chapter 7
- System Preferences: Glossary, Chapter 3
- Text-to-Speech: Chapter 8
- Time-Saving Tips: Chapter 8
- Trackpad Gestures: Chapter 3
- Touch ID: Glossary, Chapter 6
- Troubleshooting: Chapter 7
- Wi-Fi Setup: Chapter 2

This appendix offers resources and quick-reference tools to support your learning and growth as a MacBook user. With the glossary, resources, and index, you'll always have information at hand to help you deepen your knowledge, solve problems, and enhance your MacBook experience.

Conclusion

Congratulations on reaching the end of this guide! By now, you've covered a wide range of skills and features, from mastering the basics to exploring more advanced capabilities. Learning to use a MacBook can feel daunting at first, but each step you've taken brings you closer to feeling comfortable, confident, and capable with your device. Take a moment to recognize your progress—understanding and personalizing your MacBook is no small feat, and you've done an amazing job by working through each chapter, one by one.

Remember that technology is meant to be a helpful tool that adapts to your needs, not something that you need to master overnight. The skills you've learned are here to make your daily life easier, whether that's keeping in touch with loved ones, managing your schedule, or simply browsing the web. As you continue using your MacBook, you'll find that these tasks become second nature. Don't hesitate to revisit sections of this guide whenever you need a refresher; each time you do, you'll deepen your understanding and become even more fluent with your MacBook's capabilities.

As for what comes next, the possibilities are truly limitless. Your MacBook has so much to offer, and now that you're comfortable with the essentials, you're in an excellent position to explore further. Experiment with new apps, try out different customization options, and see what additional tools or features might enhance your daily routine. There's a world of possibilities within the App Store, from productivity tools to creative apps, each designed to help you accomplish your goals or provide entertainment.

Take your time, explore at your own pace, and don't be afraid to try something new. This is your MacBook, and it's here to work for you.

If you're interested in learning more, consider checking out the additional resources listed in the appendix. There, you'll find helpful websites, online communities, and other sources of information that can guide you in your ongoing journey with technology. Whether you want to refine a particular skill, troubleshoot new questions, or simply stay up to date with Apple's latest updates, there are many ways to continue growing. Learning is a lifelong process, and with the foundation you've built, you're well-equipped to tackle any tech challenge that comes your way.

Finally, I'd like to thank you for trusting this guide to help you on your journey. It's been a pleasure creating this resource with your needs in mind, and I'm grateful for the opportunity to be part of your learning experience.

If you have any feedback or would like to reach out, please don't hesitate. You can find additional resources and contact information at the back of the book, along with links to connect or access further support.

Thank you once again, and congratulations on everything you've accomplished. Enjoy your MacBook, continue exploring, and above all, have fun! The world of technology is in your hands, and you have the skills and knowledge to make the most of it.

Printed in Dunstable, United Kingdom